Econometric Models as Guides for Decision-Making

The Charles C. Moskowitz Memorial Lectures
College of Business and Public Administration
New York University

THE FREE PRESS
A Division of Macmillan Publishing Co., Inc.
NEW YORK

Collier Macmillan Publishers
LONDON

THE FREE PRESS
A Division of Macmillan Publishing Co., Inc.
866 Third Avenue, New York, N.Y. 10022

Collier Macmillan Canada, Ltd.

Library of Congress Catalog Card Number: 81-69262

Printed in the United States of America

LC

printing number
2 3 4 5 6 7 8 9 10

Library of Congress Cataloging in Publication Data

Klein, Lawrence Robert.
  Econometric models as guides for decision making.

  (The Charles C. Moskowitz memorial lectures ; no. 22)
  Includes bibliographical references and index.
  1. Econometrics--Mathematical models--Addresses, essays, lectures.   2. United States--Economic policy--1971-   --Mathematical models--Addresses, essays, lectures.   3. Economic forecasting--Mathematical models--Addresses, essays, lectures.   4. Decision-making--Mathematical models--Addresses, essays, lectures.
  I. Title. II. Series.
  HB141.K529   330'.028   81-69262
  ISBN 0-02-917430-9   AACR2

Econometric Models as Guides for Decision-Making

THE CHARLES C. MOSKOWITZ MEMORIAL
LECTURES

NUMBER XXII

Lawrence R. Klein

Benjamin Franklin Professor of
Finance and Economics
University of Pennsylvania

Nobel Laureate in Economics

DISCUSSANTS

ROBERT A. KAVESH

Marcus Nadler Professor of Finance and Economics
New York University

M. ISHAQ NADIRI

Jay Gould Professor of Economics
New York University

GARY WENGLOWSKI

Partner
Goldman, Sachs and Co.

FOREWORD

This volume, the twenty-second in the Charles C. Moskowitz Memorial Lectures series (see p. 13), is concerned with the use of econometric models as guides for decision-making. I believe most everyone would agree that econometric models are very powerful analytical instruments, and that their development has affected economic forecasting and decision-making significantly, both at the macro level of the federal government and the micro level of individual business organizations. Yet they have become a source of considerable dispute, probably less because they lack utility than because of disagreement over whether one model is better than another—that is, more accurate as a forecasting tool and guide to decision-making.

The issue takes on special significance in the context of a major shift in the orientation of economic policy in our nation. The Reagan Administration has proposed a sweeping economic program which is based on assumptions radically different from those which have for years been the foundation for economic policy decisions. According to the March 2, 1981 issue of *Business Week* (page 14) the new Administration's program is based on an econometric model constructed by John Rutledge of the Claremont Economics Institute. Mr. Rutledge, who is acting as a consultant to the Office of Management and Budget, is said to have built his model on what is known as a "rational expectations approach"—a claim with which he does not altogether agree, probably because there is serious doubt that rational expectations can be converted into mathematically quantifiable forecasts. In any case, his model has presumably been approved by Murray Weidenbaum as a basis for the new Administration's planning.

On the other hand, we have the remarkable record of economic forecasts made by the Research Seminar in Quantitative Economics, which came into being under the directorship of Professor Lawrence Klein in 1951. That record was summarized by several members of the University of Michigan's Economics Department. They said:[1]

RSQE's first Outlook Conference forecast was made by Klein in November, 1952. Twenty-eight years later . . . Klein was awarded the Nobel Prize in Economics in recognition of the significance of the econometric model-building activity which he began and to which he has made so many outstanding contributions. During these twenty-eight years of RSQE forecasting, the U.S. economy has experienced six recessions. Five of these were severe enough to produce at least one year-to-year decline in real GNP, and the 1974–75 recession produced two consecutive annual declines in real GNP. Of the six GNP declines thus visible in the annual data, RSQE forecasts made at the preceding year's Outlook Conference correctly anticipated four—including, most recently, our forecast of a decline in real GNP for the year 1980.

A somewhat amusing illustration occurs to me. In baseball a hitter with a .666 batting average is a phenomenon as yet undiscovered. Why then should an economic model with such a record for correct forecasting not lead to economic decision-making characterized by results markedly better than those presently prevailing in our country? In fact, the economists just quoted added these comments:[2]

Economists have for many years been trying to grapple with the notion of optimal policies to promote economic stability. Frankly, we have not made a great deal of progress beyond being able to raise plausible doubts about the workability of virtually every scheme that has been proposed. But plausible doubts are not proof. . . . The evident lack of success of the middle-of-the road economic policies which have characterized the past 15 years of economic turbulence in this country leaves us little basis for outright rejection of what might be a reasonably fresh look at problems which have, in truth, been getting the better of us. . .

Recognizing policy failures and poor decisions which were often based on one or another econometric model, we were fortunate indeed to have last year's Nobel Laureate in Economics as this year's Moskowitz Lecturer. Lawrence Klein has authored at least twenty books and almost 200 articles. A pioneer in applied and theoretical econometrics, he is internationally acknowledged as a leader in the development of econometric models. His paper, "Precision in Applied Economics," provides a framework within which reasonable expectations as to ranges of accuracy can be set in connection with the forecasts produced by econometric models. Of course, this leaves decision-makers with guides that are somewhat imprecise, and therefore usable only with considerable judgment and some risk—but this situation is far superior to proceeding blindly, and should not be confused with so doing.

We were fortunate too in having three distinguished economists, two of them from the academic world and one from the business arena, as discussants. They revealed a significant range of opinion in their remarks, with Professor Kavesh and Mr. Wenglowski showing somewhat greater respect for forecasts based primarily on judgment than Professor Nadiri. But all three seemed more strongly inclined to give such forecasts significant weight than did Professor Klein. In any event, the lecture paper and the comments are rich in substance and should contribute importantly to the ongoing discussion of econometric models and their usefulness in real-world decision-making.

I express appreciation to Maureen Beecher and Virginia Moress for the handling of all the arrangements for the lectures, along with Susan Landis for the editorial preparation of this volume, and to Professors Jules Backman, Ernest Bloch, and Ernest Kurnow, who constitute the faculty members of the Charles C. Moskowitz Memorial Lecture Committee. I appreciate too the work of The Free Press for the efficiency and care with which they handled the production of this small but significant volume.

Abraham L. Gitlow, Dean
College of Business and
Public Administration
New York University
May 2, 1981

Notes

1. E. P. Howrey, S. H. Hymans, H. T. Shapiro, and J. P. Crary, "The U. S. Economic Outlook for 1981," *Economic Outlook U.S.A.*, Winter 1981 (Vol. 8, No. 1), 3.
2. *Ibid.*, p. 9.

THE CHARLES C. MOSKOWITZ
MEMORIAL LECTURES

●

THE CHARLES C. MOSKOWITZ MEMORIAL LECTURES were established through the generosity of a distinguished alumnus of the College of Business and Public Administration, the late Charles C. Moskowitz of the Class of 1914.

It was Mr. Moskowitz's aim to contribute to the understanding of functional issues of major concern to business and the nation by providing a public forum for the dissemination of enlightened business theories and practices.

A pioneer in the American motion-picture industry, Charles Moskowitz worked with other innovators to create a business and entertainment phenomenon of enormous influence. He retired only after many years as Vice-President and Treasurer, and a Director, of Loew's, Inc.

This volume is the twenty-second in the Moskowitz series. The earlier ones are:

February, 1961   *Business Survival in the Sixties*
Thomas F. Patton, President and Chief
Executive Officer
Republic Steel Corporation

November, 1961   *The Challenges Facing Management*
Don G. Mitchell, President
General Telephone and Electronics
Corporation

November, 1962   *Competitive Private Enterprise Under
Government Regulation*
Malcolm A. MacIntyre, President
Eastern Air Lines

November, 1963   *The Common Market: Friend or Competitor?*
Jesse W. Markham, Professor of
Economics, Princeton University
Charles E. Fiero, Vice President,
The Chase Manhattan Bank
Howard S. Piquet, Senior Specialist in
International Economics, Legislative
Reference Service, The Library of
Congress

November, 1964   *The Forces Influencing the American
Economy*
Jules Backman, Research Professor of
Economics, New York University
Martin R. Gainsbrugh, Chief Economist and Vice President, National
Industrial Conference Board

November, 1965 *The American Market of the Future*
Arno H. Johnson, Vice President and
Senior Economist, J. Walter Thomp-
son Company
Gilbert E. Jones, President, IBM
World Trade Corporation
Darrell B. Lucas, Professor of
Marketing and Chairman of the
Department, New York University

November, 1966 *Government Wage-Price Guideposts in
the American Economy*
George Meany, President, American
Federation of Labor and Congress of
Industrial Organizations
Roger M. Blough, Chairman of the
Board and Chief Executive Officer,
United States Steel Corporation
Neil H. Jacoby, Dean, Graduate School
of Business Administration, Univer-
sity of California at Los Angeles

November, 1967 *The Defense Sector in the American
Economy*
Jacob K. Javits, United States Senator,
New York
Charles J. Hitch, President, University
of California
Arthur F. Burns, Chairman, Federal
Reserve Board

November, 1968 *The Urban Environment: How It Can
Be Improved*

William E. Zisch, Vice-chairman of the Board, Aerojet-General Corporation

Paul H. Douglas, Chairman, National Commission on Urban Problems
Professor of Economics, New School for Social Research

Robert C. Weaver, President, Bernard M. Baruch College of the City University of New York
Former Secretary of Housing and Urban Development

November, 1969   *Inflation: The Problem It Creates and the Policies It Requires*

Arthur M. Okun, Senior Fellow, The Brookings Institution

Henry H. Fowler, General Partner, Goldman, Sachs & Co.

Milton Gilbert, Economic Adviser, Bank for International Settlements

March, 1971   *The Economics of Pollution*

Kenneth E. Boulding, Professor of Economics, University of Colorado

Elvis J. Stahr, President, National Audubon Society

Solomon Fabricant, Professor of Economics, New York University
Former Director, National Bureau of Economic Research

Martin R. Gainsbrugh, Adjunct Professor of Economics, New York University

Chief Economist, National Industrial
  Conference Board

April, 1971   *Young America in the NOW World*
Hubert H. Humphrey, Senator from
  Minnesota
Former Vice President of the United
  States

April, 1972   *Optimum Social Welfare and*
Productivity: A Comparative View
Jan Tinbergen, Professor of Develop-
  ment Planning, Netherlands School
  of Economics
Abram Bergson, George E. Baker
  Professor of Economics, Harvard
  University
Fritz Machlup, Professor of Eco-
  nomics, New York University
Oskar Morgenstern, Professor of Eco-
  nomics, New York University

April, 1973   *Fiscal Responsibility: Tax Increases or*
Spending Cuts?
Paul McCracken, Edmund Ezra Day
  University, Professor of Business
  Adminstration, University of Mich-
  igan
Murray L. Weidenbaum, Edward
  Mallinckrodt Distinguished Universi-
  ty Professor, Washington University
Lawrence S. Ritter, Professor of Fi-
  nance, New York University

Robert A. Kavesh, Professor of Finance, New York University

March, 1974

Wall Street in Transition: The Emerging System and its Impact on the Economy
Henry G. Manne, Distinguished Professor of Law, Director of the Center for Studies in Law and Economics, University of Miami Law School
Ezra Solomon, Dean Witter Professor of Finance, Stanford University

March, 1975

Leaders and Followers in an Age of Ambiguity
George P. Shultz, Professor, Graduate School of Business, Stanford University
President, Bechtel Corporation

March, 1976

The Economic System in an Age of Discontinuity: Long-Range Planning or Market Reliance?
Wassily Leontief, Nobel Laureate, Professor of Economics, New York University
Herbert Stein, A. Willis Robertson Professor of Economics, University of Virginia

March, 1977

Demographic Dynamics in America
Wilber J. Cohen, Dean of the School of Education and Professor of Education and of Public Welfare Ad-

ministration, University of Michigan
Charles F. Westoff, Director of the Office of Population Research and Maurice During Professor of Demographic Studies, Princeton University

March, 1978

The Rediscovery of the Business Cycle
Paul A. Volcker, President and Chief Executive Officer, Federal Reserve Bank of New York

March, 1979

Economic Pressure and the Future of The Arts
William Schuman, Composer
Roger L. Stevens, Chairman of the Board of Trustees, John F. Kennedy Center for the Performing Arts

April, 1980

Presidential Promises and Performance
McGeorge Bundy, Professor of History, Faculty of Arts and Science, New York University
Edmund S. Muskie, Former U.S. Senator from Minnesota, Secretary of State

Note: All but the last four volumes of The Charles C. Moskowitz Memorial Lectures were published by New York University Press, 21 West Fourth Street, New York, N.Y. 10003. The 1977, 1978, 1979, and 1980 lectures were published by The Free Press.

CONTENTS

PRECISION IN APPLIED ECONOMICS

Lawrence R. Klein
Benjamin Franklin Professor
of Finance and Economics
University of Pennsylvania
Nobel Laureate in Economics

"Economic predictions are fallible and advice is highly variable."

—President Jimmy Carter
Camp David Summit
Summer 1979

Criticism

Economics is classified among the social sciences. This, I believe, is a proper identity, but how "hard" are the social sciences and should they, as a group, be labeled as arts or sciences? Words don't matter all that much, as we shall keep on doing what we have always done, but what will be expected of us?

In this essay, I want to try to give as realistic an assessment as possible about what ought to be expected, in terms of accuracy of econometric models, in particular, but this assessment is probably indicative of expectations for economics in general. To give some relevant perspective to nonspecialists or nonprofessionals, I would say that economics might rightfully be compared with meteorology. The reason for this comparison is that both subjects rely heavily

27

on data-intensive statistical investigations generated either from uncontrolled experiments or from completely nonexperimental data. As a statistical method, econometrics makes much of the assumption that information is largely (not absolutely) nonexperimental, in the sense of laboratory control. Both subjects, economics and meteorology, have a relatively low signal-to-noise ratio. The noise component that upsets meteorology is called atmospheric turbulence. In econometrics it is the residual disturbance.

Anger, frustration, and disappointment with weather forecasts are familiar assessments; similarly, economic forecasts are often off the mark. By way of comparison, weather forecasts are useful indicators for one, two, or three days in advance. They are much less useful for the month, one year, or longer horizons. The analogous time frame in economics is one, two, or three months for reliability. Perhaps, as I shall argue, one-year horizons are quite sensible for useful economic forecasting, but errors are much larger over longer stretches of time.

Short-run meteorological forecasts have significantly improved over the years, and the same is true of economic forecasts. I shall try to make this point clear during the course of this essay. Both subjects have benefitted enormously from the development and use of the high-speed electronic computer.

It has sometimes been argued that the lack of experimentation should not be cited as an obstacle to more success for economic forecasting or for the establishment of economics as a "hard" science because astronomy is also a nonexperimental science, and it is capable of making quite accurate predictions. The main difference is that the signal-to-noise ratio is very high in astronomy, much higher than in either economics or meteorology; therefore, the latter two nonexperimental sciences are more closely comparable.

Another science that may be cited for comparison is seismology. Seismological predictions are not very accurate, but this subject appears to deal with more isolated events. It, too, could be included in the comparison, but appears to me to be less relevant than meteorology.

The Role and Significance of Forecasting. When the economic policy proposals associated with the early development of Keynesian economics were first discussed—public spending, taxing, monetary control—it was recognized immediately that forecasts would be very important in determining the appropriate amounts of stimulus or restraint to be applied to the economy and in appraising the gains to be realized as a result of the policy intervention. When practitioners came up against the hard realities of economic life and found that forecasts do not always work out with a high degree of precision, many nonquantitative policy makers—certainly the noneconometricians—argued that it did not matter, after all, whether or not forecasting accuracy was attained, because policy makers could always adapt and correct any situation that reflected a poor forecast.

This is not a perceptive observation, however. It will not be possible to avoid the need for having good forecasts in order to execute proper economic policy. Hard as it may be, it will be necessary to forecast as well as possible and make use of the uncertain projections as efficiently as possible. Adaptation is easily expressed but not very well executed. It requires a great deal of skill, effort, and comradeship for the executive branch to get fast, flexible action by the legislative branch, where money bills originate. In a democratic society, it is extremely difficult to get fast enough, well-considered policy changes that are necessary to adapt to a new forecast situation. President Johnson waited more than two years to get a tax increase from Congress to pay for the Vietnam war.

A major, if not *the* major, application to econometrics is the scaling of credibility in a research team. Forecast testing is one of the most rigorous and relevant tests of a model. Predictive testing is important because objective standards for model validation, if implemented, determine credibility. If a model has not passed forecasting tests under conditions of frequent replication, the outside-user world has little to go on for judging the model's overall credibility. The main use of econometric models is likely to be in scenario analysis in the form of simulation to explore the alternatives before us.

Predictive testing is not simply the comparison of actual values for the variables generated by a model with the forecasted values when the actual readings become available after the event. It also concerns the testing for business cycle content of models, for their response characteristics, for their tendencies toward long-run equilibrium, and other criteria. A model should be examined in many different ways, against external (nonsample) information. After having passed several of the abovementioned predictive tests, credibility in the model should approach the policymaker's needs, and the validated model can then be used in the setting of economic policy and the formation of economic decisions.

People are told by politicians that they (the people) must suffer some deprivations while the policies are being implemented. If the policies are successful, it may well turn out to have been mutually advantageous. But the final verdict at the decision stage depends on whether the policy is too ambitious or not. If people are to be asked to make sacrifices they should do so only in full knowledge about what lies ahead. For, since there are many persons, each differently situated, it is essential to look over promises in the light of model validation to see whether the expected rewards outweigh the losses (setbacks) and justify the hardships.

The use of colorful euphemisms such as "projections," "scenarios," "estimates," or other synonyms for forecasts will not justify the attempts to skirt the issues. Forecasts *are* central to economic policy, and they shall be deemed accurate or inaccurate on the basis of repeated use by decisionmakers.

The present discussion about accuracy of econometric model prediction is precipitated by charges that econometric forecasts underestimated the degree of inflation that has occurred since 1973. This is a correct criticism, but the issue is not that econometric forecasts missed the magnitude of this surge in inflation; practically all economic projections, by any method whatsoever, missed it too. Econometric forecasts were quite correct in noting, as early as autumn, 1973, that inflation was going up in the United States

by significant amounts, say from 5 to 8 percent. They
did not reach as high as 12 to 15 percent.

The principal issue is that models did not prop-
erly integrate food, fuel, and flexible exchange rates
into their equation systems. Within a short period of
time, those deficiencies were rectified, and models
have, ever since, been quite perceptive in showing the
sensitivity of inflation, and other magnitudes, to
changes in food and fuel markets, with their associated repercussions on currency exchange rates. These
latter variables are also much better understood now,
after a post–Bretton Woods experience has been
established, and are incorporated into models. This
has been a learning experience for all economists.

Contrary to much casually formed opinion,
econometric models did capture the spirit of stagfla-
tion, and were able to predict that both unemployment and inflation would rise together. Disturbances
in world food and fuel markets work their way
through mainstream econometric models with stag-
flation results.

The problem, as I see it, is that people had
excessively high expectations, and looked to econometric models for very precise results. Sound econometrics should have as its objective to make appropriate estimates of signal and noise. If the ratio of
the two components is in reality low, it would be in-
correct to force the "fitting" of economic relationships to achieve high ratios; and it would be un-
reasonable for people to expect models to produce
results with high ratios when the actual economic
structure has low ratios. I believe that econometric
models indicate the appropriate ratio and that the

kinds of results that we do obtain are correct. I also believe that they are useful for decision-makers.

The failure is newsworthy, but let me cite some uncommon successes—forecasts of:

1. No return to output/employment conditions of the 1930's, immediately after World War II demobilization, 1945-46
2. A mild recession after the Korean war, 1953-54
3. A mild recession in 1969
4. A recovery with stimulus of the NEP, completed two days after the announcement of this program, August 15, 1971
5. A national and worldwide recession within one month after the imposition of the oil embargo in October, 1973
6. No recession in 1979; mild recession in 1980

The last episode is one that merits some elaboration. Each such episode has its hero. Individual followers of economic conditions are frequently cited for having called a particular turn of events. The difference between the assessment of such anecdotal evidence and the record of econometric forecasts is that the former are isolated events while the latter are replicated. The Wharton model has been projected every quarter since summer, 1963. The records have been kept and tabulated on many occasions during the 1960s and 1970s. Details of this performance will be more carefully considered in the next section, but on this occasion one anecdote on the side of model forecasts should be cited, to list another hero together with the personal heros.

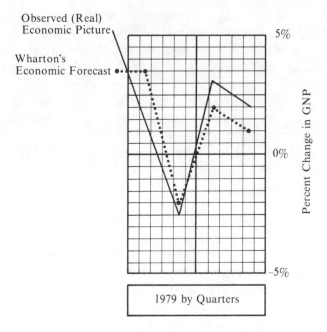

Source: Robert L. McLaughlin, "Never, Never—Repeat—NEVER Forecast Recession." *Business Economics*, XV (May, 1980), 8. Used by permission.

In an article in *Business Economics*, Robert McLaughlin notes that the Wharton model made a near-perfect forecast. Its release of December, 1978, projected the quarter-by-quarter pattern of real GNP during 1979. The accompanying graph, taken from McLaughlin's article, shows an uncanny correspondence between prediction and realization. Not only did the model operator at that time, Dr. R. M. Young, resist a widespread judgment that recession would occur during 1979, but he laid out an extremely close quarterly pattern of up-and-down movements.

During the past decade or more three challenges have been introduced against, or associated with, econometric forecasting. These three are:

1. Monetarism
2. Rational expectations
3. Supply-side effects

1. Monetarism is nothing new. The history of the quantity theory of money goes back at least to Irving Fisher, and undoubtedly has earlier roots. In an all-too-brief sense, the quantity theory introduces a single equation relating nominal income and nominal cash balances. It is based on a simple recursive structure in which the monetary authorities are assumed to control cash balances (exogenously) and thus determine nominal income by a tight-fitting single equation. The remainder of the variables describing the economy determined by a number of allocative relationships, preferably like those in a general equilibrium system of competitive market relations.

Toward the beginnning of the 1970s a number of investigators were impressed by the high correlations that they found for single-equation variants of the quantity equation, with detailed investigation of the lag structures. Like so many other impressive correlations in the history of economics, the simple quantity equation, even with good lag structure, failed to extrapolate well, especially in the period of NEP and again in the era of expensive energy pricing by OPEC. The quantity equation is uninformative about exogenous decisions by authorities, other than those affecting money supply and about conditions in raw-material or energy markets. A principal example of monetarism, the St. Louis model, broke down as far as short-run prediction of the economy is concerned, and focussed on long-term analysis. Monetarism is in political favor now in a few countries, but not by virtue of scientific validation of its predictive accuracy. The experience of the United States since the implementation of the monetary operating procedures of the Federal Reserve (October, 1979) does not even suggest that the relevant monetary aggregates can be effectively controlled. Forecasting accuracy of the monetary aggregates on the basis of control of monetary instruments has been poor, by the standards of macroeconometric model accuracy, but the experience has been short-lived, and it is too early to judge the outcome. The pure volatility of the aggregates has been extraordinarily large since October, 1979.

2. The earliest econometric models of the postwar period (ever since 1945) have been specified in terms of expected values, especially for prices and incomes. Generally speaking, an expected value was expressed as estimated weighted sums of own past values; in other words, as lag distributions. An important advance was made, however, with the combined use of sample survey methods and aggregative time-series analysis, by introducing direct estimates of price expectations, income expectations purchase plans, and other personal attitudes. This approach has been used both for the household and the enterprise sectors of the economy.

Rational expectations methods continue along this well-established line of research by arguing that own lag distributions are inadequate representations of expected values, and introduce in principle a whole

Table 1. Quarterly Changes in Monetary Aggregates (percent)

	M1A	*M1B*	*M2*
1976.1	5.59	5.81	13.63
2	5.94	6.49	13.32
3	3.34	3.96	11.73
4	7.17	7.78	16.06
1977.1	9.19	9.63	14.40
2	6.93	7.14	11.71
3	6.10	6.61	9.96
4	8.61	9.04	10.07
1978.1	7.82	8.11	7.74
2	8.95	9.42	7.72
3	7.25	7.52	8.45
4	5.71	7.66	9.72
1979.1	0.15	4.90	6.81
2	7.42	10.77	10.64
3	8.04	9.99	11.12
4	4.62	5.01	7.25
1980.1	4.90	6.06	7.43
2	−3.84	−2.34	5.59
3	11.45	14.21	16.43
4	8.64	11.32	9.33

SOURCE: Federal Reserve data.

spectrum of proxies for the formation of expectations—none as relevant, in my opinion, as the direct use of survey responses by the economic decision-makers themselves. The survey method puts "people" directly into the model structure. This is all very well and in the spirit of improving research methods, but the leap in reasoning by the exponents of rational expectations—to argue that expectations are functions of policy instruments in such a way that the effects of changes in these instruments are nullified by decision-makers' revised action—seems to me to be wholly unjustified. It seems to be a contrived argument to show that macroeconomic policy is futile. It has no independent empirical justification. In some versions of this theory it has been asserted that the parameters of macroeconometric models are functions of policy instruments and depend on those variables in just such a way as to nullify policy action. It can be agreed that the variable-parameter model generalizes the fixed-parameter model, but, as with many generalizations, it gives less specific results; and again I would repeat that there is no empirical basis for making the parameters functions of the policy instruments, let alone making them very particular functions.

The challenge of rational expectations is actually addressed to macroeconomic analysis in general and not necessarily to macroeconometric forecasting, but, since the latter activity is so prominent in the whole field of macroeconomics, there have been numerous attempts to direct the challenge toward the specification of the models presently in widespread use. I would return the challenge and ask the proponents of rational expectations to lay before professional bodies their accuracy numbers to be compared with those that I shall cite in the next section.

3. "Supply-side economics" can mean many things. In December, 1977, I presented a presidential address to the American Economic Association entitled "The Supply Side." In a single sentence, "supply-side economics" means, according to that account, the fusing of the Keynes–Leontief system—*i.e.*, a large, detailed model that combines interindustrial flows with final demand and income generation. This system should be supplemented by

detailed demographic, resource, financial, and quality-of-life modules. These all affect the conditions of supply within the economy.

A more recent and vulgar interpretation of supply-side economics asserts, without empirical validation, that direct-tax rates strongly affect worker motivation and desires to save. In principle, these effects may exist, and there is some empirical evidence for moderately favorable reactions to large-scale tax cuts for both labor supply and savings, but that is a small part of the total meaning of the supply side.

The latest renditions of supply-side economics are not challenges to macroeconometric modelling or forecasting; they are challenges to existing mainstream models to introduce more specific supply-side reactions, especially toward the incentive effects of marginal tax rates. The outcome may well be a more careful and exhaustive study for uncovering the existence of such supply-side effects. In the same vein, the principal contributions of the monetarist and rational-expectations schools have been to steer model-builders toward more careful treatment of the financial sector and the formation of expectations. It will be argued below that there are no panaceas for making an order-of-magnitude improvement in forecasting accuracy; and, at best, the improvements that may be gained as a result of the stimulation generated by these challenges will make some modest improvements in overall accuracy.

Another criticism of econometric forecasting has been not of its accuracy, but a charge that the attained accuracy has been a result of man–model interaction and not based entirely on the model itself. There are fundamental reasons why an estimated model cannot be used in a mechanical arithmetic way for forecasting. Data are repeatedly being revised. The sample data for model estimation are sure to be changed by the time forecast application arrives. The high-speed computer enables us to reduce this discrepancy through recomputation, but not to eliminate it except by using very small models which have their own deficiencies, as in the case of the quantity equation.

A second reason for human intervention in model application for forecasting is that statutory changes alter the structure of the system in an approximate way, and external disturbances such as wars, strikes, embargoes, droughts, earthquakes, floods, and other large environmental events upset the working of parts of the economic system, often temporarily. Finally, there are drifts in behavior that tend to be serial but temporary and not apparent in the sample period.

Typical forecast exercises adjust models so as to align their performance with initial conditions, last-minute fragmentary information, and external (non-sample) information about events to come. This is an efficient use of models. The main reactions are kept intact for policy analyses after adjustments have been made. Application in this form, judged particularly by the forecast record, have been superior to pure model applications or pure human-judgment applications. I would assert that man–model forecasts are better than either purist forecast.

The Record

It is not possible to summarize recorded performance in a single sentence or even in a normal paragraph. It is a complicated matter that must be looked at in many dimensions. The fact that the econometric forecasting industry has been, and still is, a growth sector in the private economy attests to its having had a successful market test, but from a scholarly academic viewpoint other criteria need to be developed.

Since 1963, quarterly records of Wharton forecasts have been maintained, and since 1970 annual projections by our versions of the Keynes–Leontief system have been established; but in this section I am going to focus on published documentation developed by third-party analysts, the most "official" of which are those published by Stephen McNees in various issues of the *New England Economic Review*. He has produced forecast accuracy records for several mainstream models in comparison with average judgment determined from median forecasts of an American Statistical Association panel. McNees' tabulations show many interesting characteristics.

1. Forecast errors of *levels* grow significantly as the length of the forecast horizon grows, but forecast errors of change do not grow as much with horizon length for some variables.
2. Forecasts before 1974 were more reliable than those after 1974. The turbulent period of the second half (or two thirds) of the 1970s was very difficult for forecasters, especially in projecting inflation.
3. In the short run, the ASA judgmental forecasts are as accurate as the model forecasts, but for longer horizons the model forecasts are better.

Table 2. Mean Absolute Errors, Wharton and ASA Median Forecasts (Quarterly, 1971–79)

Quarterly Horizon	Level						Change					
	1	2	3	4	5	6	1	2	3	4	5	6
GNP Price Deflator (1972: 100, index points)												
ASA	0.4	0.8	1.4	1.9	2.7	—	0.4	0.5	0.7	0.6	0.9	—
Wharton	0.3	0.8	1.3	1.7	2.3	3.0	0.3	0.5	0.7	0.7	0.8	0.8
Mid-Quarter Wharton	0.3	0.6	1.2	1.7	2.3	3.0	0.3	0.5	0.7	0.7	0.8	0.8
Real GNP (billions of 1972 dollars)												
ASA	7.0	10.2	13.7	17.4	22.0	—	7.0	9.8	10.2	10.1	10.5	—
Wharton	7.8	11.2	13.4	17.1	22.0	25.8	7.8	9.6	10.3	10.0	11.6	11.5
Mid-Quarter Wharton	7.0	11.0	12.7	17.2	21.0	25.6	7.0	9.9	9.0	10.3	10.7	11.4
Unemployment Rate (percentage points)												
ASA	0.1	0.3	0.4	0.5	0.7	—	0.1	0.2	0.2	0.2	0.2	—
Wharton	0.2	0.4	0.5	0.6	0.6	0.7	0.2	0.2	0.2	0.2	0.2	0.3
Mid-Quarter Wharton	0.1	0.4	0.5	0.6	0.6	0.7	0.1	0.3	0.3	0.2	0.2	0.3
Money Supply, M1 (billions of current dollars)												
Wharton	1.6	2.9	4.2	5.0	5.7	6.2	1.6	1.9	1.7	1.9	1.7	1.5
Mid-Quarter Wharton	1.3	2.3	3.4	4.7	5.6	6.0	1.3	1.7	1.6	1.8	1.7	1.6
Treasury Bill Rate (percentage points)												
Wharton	0.2	0.7	1.2	1.5	1.7	1.9	0.2	0.6	0.6	0.6	0.6	0.0
Mid-Quarter Wharton	0.2	0.7	1.2	1.5	1.7	1.8	0.2	0.6	0.7	0.6	0.6	0.7

SOURCE: Stephen K. McNees, "The Forecasting Record for the 1970's," *New England Economic Review* (September/October, 1979), 33–53. Used by permission.

Table 3. Mean Absolute Error of Growth Rates, Wharton Model

Quarterly Horizon	1	2	3	4	5	6
Change Forecast						
Final Sales	2.5	2.5	2.4	2.3	2.4	2.7
Personal Consumption, Nondurables	1.8	1.8	2.1	2.2	2.2	2.2
Personal Consumption, Durables	10.2	11.5	12.7	11.3	12.5	12.6
Residential Investment	11.8	15.0	15.3	17.9	20.0	20.1
Business Fixed Investment	6.4	7.9	6.8	6.6	7.5	7.2

SOURCE: Stephen K. McNees, *op. cit.* Used by permission.

This is not uniform, but holds for some leading aggregates.

4. Highly variable magnitudes such as investment in fixed capital, residential real estate, and inventories have relatively large errors.

5. The Wharton mid-quarter forecasts are generally better than early-quarter forecasts for leading variables—even for longer horizons, far away from the current quarter. This provides evidence about the efficiency of man–model forecasts, since the mid-quarter projections are made with the benefit of an exhaustive two-day critique by external users of the forecast.

6. The different man–model forecast teams do not differ markedly among themselves, but they do have a record that is far superior to that compiled by mechanistically applied models. The similarity of the records of man-model teams as the people change over successive generations of human-forecast operators suggests that present techniques are systematized and capable of being handed on to successors; they are not purely *ad hominem*, as are pure judgmental forecasts.

How good are these estimates as judged by Dr. McNees' error statistics? Various comparisons have been established between accuracy of model forecasts and those of purely mechanical schemes, not to mention the comparison with average judgment cited already. One interesting comparison is between the error of model forecasts and the degree of data revision by those who compile the basic economic statistics. Economic data, as already pointed out, are "noisy." They are often being changed on the basis of new observational information. Given all the insight and inside information possessed by the data collection/publication agencies—in this case, the national income division of the United States Department of Commerce—one could not expect the model-builder to do better in projection than this group does in observation measurement. This, I submit, is a fundamental reason why we may not be able to make significant improvements in asymptotic efficiency. We may already be there, as Paul Samuelson conjectures (see below). In 90 percent of the cases (quarterly estimates, 1964–79), model projections one year ahead are about as close as preliminary estimates (15–20 days after a quarter's end) are to revisions that take place in the following July. The model projections appear to be closer when the third successive July revision is compared with the preliminary estimate.

Thus, 90 percent of the cases of revision of real GNP growth are revised in the range of -1.8% to 2.0 percentage points, between the first July revision. If the third July revision is compared with the preliminary figures, the range for real GNP jumps to -2.1 to 3.4 percentage points.

Table 4. Revision in Quarter-to-Quarter Percent Changes (Annual Rate)

		Range Between Percentiles
		5% to 95%
Constant Dollar GNP	First July	−1.8 to 2.0
	Third July	−2.1 to 3.4
GNP Implicit Price Deflator	First July	−0.8 to 1.5
	Third July	−0.7 to 1.9

SOURCE: Department of Commerce

The Wharton model forecast appears to be favorable in error performance, relative to one year accuracy in compiling some of the basic data. The range of correction of the price data are similar to the accuracy of model forecasting of the same magnitude. Up to the first July the range is between −0.8 percentage points and ±1.5 percentage points. These ranges (90 percent probability) correspond fairly well with Dr. McNees' tabulations with these data.

The tabulations by McNees do not throw light on the critical issue of behavior of error in the neighborhood of turning points. It is well known that turning-point errors tend to be larger than errors in the other phases of the cycle. It is generally easier to rack up good error statistics during protracted expansion or contraction phases because the serial aspect of economic behavior is abundantly represented in the smooth lag distributions of model specification. Results reported by Vincent Su show that the margin of superiority of Wharton model forecasts over ASA median forecasts is decidedly greater at turning points, especially in the ability to call the turn in advance.[1] He found the mid-quarter Wharton forecasts to be better than the month-earlier forecasts in calling the turn.

The matter of superiority of models over judgmental forecasts could be extended to cover pure time-series forecasts, as well. Time-series methods should do as well as models for very short horizons, up to three or possibly six months, but time-series methods tend to cumulate error rapidly and deteriorate markedly after three- to six-month horizons.[2] The disadvantage of both time-series and judgmental methods is that they do not provide for rapid generation of forecast alternatives. A principal reason for careful evaluation of forecast error and attempting to do as well as possible in *ex ante* forcasting is to build up a credibility record so that policy alternatives may be studied on the basis of validated models. That is surely one of the most important applications (policy alternatives), more important in many respects than pure generation of forecasts. Credibility is established on the basis of replication because successful *ex ante* prediction is not likely to be possible if repeated over and over again, unless the model has a good degree of reliability.

It is not only error accumulation caused by the propagation process of time-series methods that causes rapid fading of forecasts by that approach, but also an inability to build exogenous changes into a system's structure. Much of the success of macro-econometric forecasting stems from an ability to build in large exogenous swings such as those that occurred with NEP in 1971 and the oil embargo of 1973. Time-series methods would be uninformative about the effects of these unique events.

In summarizing some of his tabulations, McNees writes:

> If no other set of forecasts was systematically more accurate, these performances, while not ideal—no forecaster was gifted with perfect foresight—would represent the *minimum feasible* errors for forecasts of the 1970s.
>
> The forecasts examined above must be considered "good" until other forecasters document that it was possible to have produced systematically more accurate predictions.

To me, this remark indicates that main man–model forecasts stand as the best available device until something superior is found that can be used on a replicated basis. Two other commentators at the American Economic Association meeting of December, 1977, when Su's results were reported, noted that models had their errors, but

> . . . they are the work of professionals and should be called upon when professional forecasting is needed, in the same way that a plumber is called when a serious leak needs fixing.
>
> —(the late) Arthur Okun
>
> . . . models genuinely add something to our forecasting ability that is not present in other methods.
>
> —Victor Zarnowitz

An econometric model is a smoothing or averaging device that will tend to miss the amplitude of "spiky" movements of economic series at their extremes. In other words, economists tend to underpredict the absolute value of change. Model operators tend to be conservative, and this introduces another factor in their not picking out the full magnitude of change. Large increases in the rate of inflation were predicted in autumn, 1973, but they were not large enough. The actual increases would have seemed to be incredible at the time, and econometricians would not have been believed if they had projected inflation of 12 percent instead of 8 percent for 1974.

The tendency to underpredict change is partly responsible for missing the magnitude of inflation in recent years and also for doing more poorly in the turbulent part of the last decade than in the earlier part.

It is customary to look over the correspondences between actual and forecast values of the endogenous variables of an econometric model in judging accuracy, but another group of variables, the exogenous variables, may also be tabulated for forecast comparison. Exogenous variables constitute input values for the calculation of forecasts. The exogenous variables go with the model, and it is meaningful to look into their forecast accuracy, too. It may be possible to construct models that depend on hard-to-predict exogenous variables, and the lack of success in forecasting the exogenous variables may have significant impact on the accuracy of the entire forecast.

Strategic exogenous variables are public expenditures and revenues.

Table 5. Estimated and Actual Federal Budget Revenues (NIPA), 1974–1980 (Billions of Dollars, Wharton Model)

Calendar Year	Forecast Value*	Actual	Difference	
			Dollars	Percent
1974	287.3	287.8	− .5	− 0
1975	318.9	287.3	31.6	11
1976	337.1	331.7	5.4	2
1977	375.3	375.1	0.2	0
1978	409.5	431.4	− 21.9	− 5
1979	467.0	494.4	− 27.4	− 6
1980	530.7	539.7	− 9.0	− 2
Average absolute difference			13.7	3.7

*Forecast value was obtained from previous year November Post-Meeting Control Solution
SOURCE: Wharton EFA

Table 6. Estimated and Actual Federal Budget Expenditures (NIPA), 1974–1980 (Billions of Dollars, Wharton Model)

Calendar Year	Forecast Value*	Actual	Difference	
			Dollars	Percent
1974	293.0	299.3	− 6.3	− 2
1975	333.9	356.6	− 22.7	− 6
1976	405.3	384.8	20.5	5
1977	426.7	421.5	5.2	1
1978	469.4	460.7	8.7	2
1979	507.6	509.2	− 1.6	− 0
1980	573.8	601.3	− 27.5	− 5
Average absolute difference			13.2	3.0

*Forecast value was obtained from previous year November Post-Meeting Control Solution
SOURCE: Wharton EFA

Table 7. Estimated and Actual State and Local Government Revenues (NIPA), 1974-1980 (Billions of Dollars, Wharton Model)

Calendar Year	Forecast Value*	Actual	Difference	
			Dollars	Percent
1974	210.4	211.3	− 0.9	− 0
1975	226.5	237.7	− 11.2	− 5
1976	260.6	267.8	− 7.2	− 3
1977	289.2	298.0	− 8.8	− 3
1978	320.7	327.4	− 6.7	− 2
1979	352.9	351.1	1.8	0
1980	386.6	382.9	3.7	1
Average absolute difference			5.8	2.0

*Forecast value was obtained from previous year November Post-Meeting Control Solution

SOURCE: Wharton EFA

Table 8. Estimated and Actual State and Local Government Expenditures (NIPA), 1974-1980 (Billions of Dollars, Wharton Model)

Calendar Year	Forecast Value*	Actual	Difference	
			Dollars	Percent
1974	205.7	204.5	1.2	1
1975	227.4	232.2	− 4.8	− 2
1976	246.4	251.2	− 4.8	− 2
1977	273.9	270.0	3.9	1
1978	297.7	298.4	− 0.7	0
1979	330.0	324.4	5.6	2
1980	361.4	354.7	6.7	2
Average absolute difference			4.0	1

*Forecast value was obtained from previous year November Post-Meeting Control Solution

SOURCE: Wharton EFA

Table 9. Estimated and Actual Budget Receipts, 1963-1978 (Billions of Dollars)

Fiscal Year	Budget Estimate*	Actual	Difference Dollars	Percent
1963	113.5	106.6	6.9	+ 6
1964	109.3	112.7	− 3.4	− 3
1965	115.9	116.8	− 0.9	− 1
1966	119.8	130.9	− 11.1	− 8
1967	141.4	149.6	− 8.2	− 5
1968	163.3	153.7	9.6	+ 6
1969	178.1	187.8	− 9.7	− 5
1970	198.7	193.7	5.0	+ 3
1971	202.1	188.4	13.7	+ 7
1972	217.6	208.6	9.0	+ 4
1973	220.8	232.2	− 11.4	− 5
1974	256.0	264.9	− 8.9	− 3
1975	295.0	281.0	14.0	+ 5
1976	297.5	300.0	− 2.5	− 1
1977	351.3	357.8	− 6.5	− 2
1978	393.0	402.0	− 9.0	− 2
Average absolute difference			8.1	4

*Until 1977, the federal fiscal year began in July, six months after the initial estimates were published in the Budget, and ended eighteen months later. The fiscal year now runs from October 1 to September 30, thus beginning nine months after the revenue estimates are published in the Budget.

SOURCE: Office of Management and Budget, *Budget of the United States Government*, various years

The latter may be largely estimated from tax equations; so they are only partly exogenous. Tables 5 through 8 show comparisons between forecast and actual values over the past seven years, using the Wharton model. At the federal level, the average absolute errors of forecast are 3.7 and 3.0 percent, while at the state/local level the corresponding figures are 2.0 and 1.4 percent, respectively. The figures for revenue forecasts by the Office of Management and Budget (Table 9) is also about 4.0 percent; thus, we can say that model-builders have the same degree of accuracy as the official budget agency, where all the details and know-how originate. This serves as a good standard for judging predictability of these exogenous inputs in models. On the basis of this comparison, I would conclude that the Wharton Model Group do all right in their exogenous assumptions, this remark in spite of the fact that the period covered in the comparison differs between the model tables and the offical public tables.

Prospects

Paul Samuelson has said, "But I feel almost as if there is a Heisenberg Indeterminacy principle dogging us, which will limit the asymptotic accuracy of forecasting we shall be able to attain."[3] An interpretation of Samuelson's remark may be that a limit on the improvement of economic forecasts is provided by the inherent error of observation in the magnitude that is being projected. We cannot reduce an existing error level of 1 percent in forecasting real GNP if real GNP cannot be observed with less than 1 percent error. Limitations are more serious for other magnitudes. Samuelson may well be right that we have reached the asymptotic level of accuracy that is to be achieved.

I do not believe that enormous gains are going to be possible to achieve, *i, e.*, that existing error levels can be halved. There are, indeed, improvements to be made, but they are likely to be more in the neighborhood of 5 to 10 percent rather than dramatic decreases in error variance. Consider, for example, the analogy with meteorology. Through careful analysis, painstaking data collection, and heavy computation, French meteorologists believe that they can lengthen the effective time horizon of credible forecasts by a few hours in a twenty-two-day span.[4] Similarly, econometricians might be able to stretch a year's forecast horizon by about one month for a given degree of accuracy, after the input of laborious effort over a fairly long period of time.

The kinds of errors that we now make are vastly smaller than we ever dreamed possible in 1945, when we embarked on the first postwar efforts at econometric model construction. Along the way, we thought from time to time that there would be some breakthroughs, but there were no panaceas. Dreary empirical research over the years with improved data bases, better statistical methods, better analysis of the functioning of the economy, better hardware, and better software have all contributed to the achievement of today's potential. When we consider the development of these activities in other countries that started somewhat later than in the United States (or the Netherlands), we notice that they quickly rise to the U.S. standard of accuracy and then remain fairly steady on that level.

Where are some improvements to be made? In 1945, those of us at the Cowles Commission (University of Chicago) thought that better statistical methods, particularly through the application of simultaneous equation methods of estimation, would be important in improving the quality of our models. We learned a great deal about our subject through that experience and learned how to interpret models, but we did not realize large gains in accuracy as a result of the application of advanced methods of inference then being developed. The later introduction of new approaches to the estimation of distributed lags, with heavy computer input, gave us much better grasp of model dynamics, and this has contributed to forecasting improvement.

The use of survey data, especially for investment intentions, and the development of man–model interactions have both helped. The extensive use of quarterly data and survey data helped, but did not provide breakthroughs. The development of large systems of several hundred or a few thousand equations, made possible only through the use of the computer, did not contribute so much to overall accuracy of the main economic aggregates, but they did provide much more information and made the forecasts much more useful and usable. Insofar as the large systems provided for the explicit embedding of key sectors, such as energy, financial markets, agriculture, trade, and the like, they led to forecast improvement on specific occasions when big events occurred, as in the first oil crisis associated with the embargo.

A promising line of statistical research that is relatively unexploited is the introduction of variable parameters—either randomly variable, time variable, or systematically variable according to some endogenous economic principles. Successful exploitation of this line of analysis will involve both statistical method and economic theoretical specification. Generally speaking, advances in economic theory may help with specification to the point at which forecast improvements can be realized. Given our relatively small samples, economic theoretic restrictions as in consumer expenditure or production systems should enable us to enrich the spectrum of the set of explanatory variables so that many strategic cross-effects are captured well enough to improve forecast accuracy. In a sense, this can be looked upon as a technique with variable parameters or nonlinear parameters.

In practice, decision-makers use models as pieces of evidence, among many others, in coming to a conclusion for action. The typical public official summons a number of professional economists around a table and asks for estimates. Some are submitted judgmentally, intuitively, or on the basis of elaborate model projections. The policymaker sifts the evidence from all sources and makes a decision, rarely on the basis of a single source. Among different models or systematic quantitative methods a weighted combination may provide better forecasts than any one taken alone. This, too, is a promising research area.

There are some avenues of research that may lead to improvements in accuracy; nevertheless, forecast we must, and the degree of achievable accuracy is something that we shall have to learn to live with. We cannot expect, in economics, to be within small error bands—

1.5% for change in real GNP
2.0% for inflation
½ percentage point for unemployment
150 basis points for short-term interest rates
5.0 billion for the change in either internal or external deficit

—ninety-five percent of the time. We might *aspire* to be within these bands two-thirds of the time, but we should not try to adopt the conventional confidence coefficients of other branches of statistics. It would not be realistic.

Accepting these errors and suitable frequencies, it would be healthier if economic forecasts were provided in probabilistic intervals. On several occasions, relevant errors have been estimated and tabulated, but prevailing practice is to provide only point estimates, with a number of decimal places. That exceeds the limits of our precision.

Notes

1. Vincent Su, "An Error Analysis of Econometric and Non-econometric Forecasts," *American Economic Review*, 68 (May, 1978), 306–12.
2. See A. A. Hirsch, Bruce T. Grimm, and Gorti V. L. Narasimham, "Some Multiplier and Error Characteristics of the BEA Quarterly Model," *Econometric Model Performance*, L. R. Klein and E. Burmeister, eds. (Philadelphia: University of Pennsylvania Press, 1976), 232–47.
3. Paul A. Samuelson, "The Art and Science of Macromodels over 50 Years," *The Brookings Model: Perspective and Recent Developments*, G. Fromm and L. R. Klein, eds. (Amsterdam: North–Holland, 1975), 3–10.
4. Daniel Cadet, Billes Sommeria, and Olivier Talagrand, "Why It's So Tough to Predict the Weather," *CNRS Research* (May 1977), 22–28.

DISCUSSANT

Robert A. Kavesh
Marcus Nadler Professor
of Finance and Economics
Graduate School
of Business Administration
New York University

Lawrence Klein is eminently qualified to discuss the uses (and abuses) of econometric models for forecasting and other decision-making. He was (and is) the pioneer in the development of large-scale macro models. Truly, he is the "King of Forecasters," and the world has taken note of his achievements by awarding him a Nobel Prize in Economic Science.

His work has created hundreds of jobs for economists and statisticians and contributed to the (until recently) rising respect in which economists were held. Every *major* macroeconomic forecasting model that is widely sold and reported upon—Chase, DRI and Wharton—was developed from his continuing researches over more than thirty years.

But these are troubled times, and new thoughts and ideas are challenging the conventional wisdom of the past half-century. The role of government, the

59

primacy of the market mechanism, the degree of regulation—these and more are being debated and acted upon in an environment of change and turmoil. Given these shifts in philosophy and sentiment, it is not surprising that the standard-bearers of the "traditional" Keynesian macro models have come under sharp attack.

Mythology repeatedly recounts the practice of regicide, which Mary Renault describes in *The King Must Die.* Sir James G. Frazer, in *The Golden Bough*, detailed the practice of puttings kings to death (or unseating them) if their health, judgment, or accuracy started decline. Freud, too, in *Totem and Taboo*, ranged over this fascinating area.

Lawrence Klein is the king: What are the new challenges? How is he responding to them? Taking them on, one by one, Dr. Klein summarizes the positions of:

1. The Monetarists
2. The Rational Expectationists
3. The Supply-Siders

In a basically even-handed fashion he deflates the exaggerated claims made by these would-be usurpers. One can sense the morality fable aspects of the debate: John Rutledge of the Claremont Economic Institute shouting a new, simpler message of incentives and tax cuts; Michael Evans, the apostate, proclaiming that only he has the "truth"; Ray Fair, the pure-model builder, refusing to "massage" the output while proving that nice guys finish last.

Lot of contenders, lots of turmoil. One thing is certain: Model-building will never be the same again. Dr. Klein describes how the "best" of the new is being blended with the "old" to produce superior models and forecasts.

One can only hope that he is right, although the dismal forecasting record for 1980 and early 1981 makes one wonder. *Every* major model was very wide of the mark during these periods. Not even the "judgmentalists"—those users of pencils and yellow sheets—did any better. It was another one of those periods of sharp discontinuity, the bane of every forecaster's existence.

A few salient findings emerge from a quarter-century of record-keeping and comparing:

1. Forecasting is not yet a "science," it's generally an "art"; occasionally a "hazard." In recent years, errors have increased rather than decreased. Nor is there very much cause for "optimism" (defined as "accuracy") in the newer models.

2. Lots of forecasting is for fun and games—to win prizes for GNP accuracy—rather than for real use in the business world. Part of this stems from the mystique of economics: A company needs a staff of economists to be considered "modern." I have a feeling that government users of models have relied much more heavily upon them than have business users.

3. On the face of it there would seem to be a methodological split between the forecasting factions represented by the formalists (econometricians) on the one hand, and the "guessers" (judgmentalists) on the other. However, the differences are more apparent than real. Econometricians adjust their results, utilizing considerable "judgment" in finally issuing forecasts (replicability, indeed!); while most judgmentalists acknowledge that they peek at the computer printouts of the formalists while filling in

their own estimates. Judgment necessarily underlies both approaches.

"Judgment," however, is a much-abused term. To many it is a substitute for analysis, a means to cover up gaps in personal knowledge. At its worst it is an invitation to whimsy and conjecture rather than an adjunct to sound, rigorous thinking. The true exercise of judgment in business forecasting is an art, but like most arts its practice can be improved by study and experience. Ultimately, then, much of what may pass for judgment is, in truth, a distillation of considerable hard work and a reliance upon a sound methodological framework. And, in this sense, it would be accurate to say that the productive forecaster relies heavily upon judgment in trying to narrow the range of uncertainty in which decisions are made.

And so, is Lawrence Klein's crown seriously threatened by the onslaught of events and conceptual developments? Perhaps—but the jury is still out and the debate will undoubtedly rage for many years. What no one can deny is the debt we all owe to this man: an intellectual debt and a moral debt—for he is truly a good man.

In Goethe's *Faust* the relevant words are spoken in the Prologue in Heaven by the Lord:

> While Man's desires and aspirations stir,
> He cannot choose but err.

and, a bit later on:

> A good man, through obscurest aspiration,
> Has still an instinct of the one true way.

DISCUSSANT

M. Ishaq Nadiri
Jay Gould Professor
of Economics
Faculty of Arts and Science
New York University

Professor Klein has provided us with a cogent and strong defense of the forecast performance of the macroeconometric models. He argues that these models have predicted well most of the business cycle developments of the postwar period, especially the levels of GNP. When dramatic changes such as the inflationary upsurge of 1973 and its aftermath occurred, these models were easily amended and their forecasting abilities were easily restored.

He takes issue with the recent challenges by the monetarist schools, proponents of the rational expectations, and the so-called supply-side economists, suggesting that these challenges do not amount to a great deal on empirical grounds. He also defends the procedure of man–model interaction, which is often practiced in forecasting circles to improve the forecast accuracy of the models. This practice is of course necessary, in order to account for unanticipated changes in policy, revisions of data, and relevant information that forecasters may have obtained. This practice does have the advantage of improving the forecasts.

Professor Klein compares the record of Wharton Econometric Model with that of ASA/NBER judgmental forecasts and finds that the model forecasts are better than those based on judgmental surveys, especially for longer horizons. Finally, he reaches a rather pessimistic conclusion that prospects for substantial improvement in forecasting performance of the econometric models may not be possible. He cautions us against excessive expectations: There are inherent errors of observation in the magnitudes of the variables that are being forecast which limit our ability to forecast them except within small error-bands. He conjunctures that we may "have reached the asymptotic level of accuracy that is to be achieved."

Instead of elaborating on points that Professor Klein and I agree on, I would like to briefly make the following observations.

1. I feel that the comparison of the econometric model forecasts with the ASA judgmental forecasts is somewhat misleading. Forecasts not based on formal econometric models appear to be generally as accurate as, and sometimes more accurate than, econometrically based forecasts. Further, there is an interplay between these two types of forecasts; the members of the ASA/NBER panel are undoubtedly influenced by the forecasts of econometric models; and, conversely, the econometric forecasting group (perhaps in their man–model interaction phase) assimilate the informal forecasters' gist of surveys,

data, and policy analysis. It should be noted that
ASA's judgmental forecasts do somewhat poorly
against Wharton Econometric Model forecasts, but
not necessarily against most of the other econometric
models.

There are, however, two advantages to the econometric models that should be noted. One is that the
noneconometric forecasts cannot be generated quickly; they are derived from cumbersome and time-consuming procedures. Also, their forecasts are often
not very comprehensive in their coverage. Another
advantage of formal econometric models is that the
sources of forecast errors can be traced, and the impact points of a policy or an exogeneous shock can be
readily identified. However, the danger does exist
that the models may cease to forecast well if there is a
major policy change.

2. I have the same apprehensions about the
monetarist school and rational-expectation proponents as Professor Klein when it comes to their contributions to econometric modeling and forecasts.
However, there are some issues that require consideration. First, it is not quite appropriate to compare the results of large-scale econometric models
such as Wharton's with simple models based on
quantity theory of money (such as the St. Louis
model). They are very simplistic, as Professor Klein
has suggested, and their poor performance is not
totally unexpected. A more appropriate comparison
ought to be with more elaborate econometric models
based on monetarist doctrine that are currently in
operation, mainly in a few large banks.

The strong version of rational expectation suggests that if expectations depend on all available information, including information about the likely course of monetary and fiscal policy, then systematic, and therefore predictable, activist policies can have no predictable real effects, even in the short run. This theory rests on two (among many others) strong assumptions. One is the assumption of continuous market-clearing equilibrium—*i. e.*, perfect price flexibility—and the other is the specification of imperfections and asymmetrics in the information on which economic agents act and form expectations.

These basic assumptions certainly do not hold in the real world, at least in the short run. The existence of implicit and explicit contracts prevalent in the economy, and the heterogeneity of products and factor services that characterizes a real economy, make continuous market-clearing impossible. The rational-expectation model requires people to know more about the operation of the economy, and about data it continuously generates, than is realistically possible.

Finally, whatever the merits of the rational-expectations argument that stabilization policy cannot influence real aggregate output in the short run, it is still possible that an activist policy may change the composition of output—such as increasing the share of investment, which has implications for future growth.

Besides these theoretical shortcomings there is not very much empirical evidence, as Professor Klein correctly states, on the validity of the rational-expectation policy prognoses. I should like, however, to note that, because of the debate on rational expectation, we may be moving toward a synthesis that will be important for macroeconometric modelling. That is, active policies may still work for traditional reasons, but less powerfully and predictably because the stabilization policy is not a "game" against nature but against intelligent agents whose reactions depend on policy moves. The challenge would be to translate *fully* this theoretical synthesis into econometric modelling. Such an effort may even lead to improvement and understanding of the forecasts of the macroeconometric models.

3. As to the future prospect for forecasting by econometric model, I remain a bit more optimistic. The principal challenge to short-term forecasting is to improve the methods for predicting turning-points; more vigorous effort to incorporate expectations of the household, of business, and especially of policy-makers may improve the forecast performance of these models. Use of variable-parameter estimation techniques, as Professor Klein has suggested, may be another possibility. Better disaggregations would be another avenue to follow. However, a major source of improvement may be not in better and more powerful estimation techniques, though it will help, but improvements in the quality of data used in econometric models. This is a point which unfortunately was not stressed in Professor Klein's presentation. As a profession, we spend too little effort measuring accurately the variables of our models, and this underinvestment may be one source of our frustrations in economic analysis and forecasting.

DISCUSSANT

Gary Wenglowski
Partner
Goldman, Sachs and Co.

Since I was a student of Professor Klein's in econometrics and am now a judgmental forecaster (no cause-and-effect is implied), I would like to focus my discussion on those parts of the lecture related to the relative merits of model-based forecasting approaches as compared to judgment-based techniques. The difference between these two main approaches to forecasting is a matter of emphasis. In the model-based approach, the model and its results are the focus, with adjustments based on judgment playing an ancillary role. In judgmental forecasting, models and their results are viewed as only one of several inputs to forming a forecasting conclusion.

I would make three points in evaluating the merits of these two approaches. First, the forecasting records of the two methods are very similar, leaving little basis to choose between them on relative accuracy. Professor Klein points out that model results tend to be more accurate as the forecast horizon lengthens. However, for the first six quarters of the forecast period analyzed on Table 2 of the lecture, the average absolute error of the judgmental forecasters was less than that of the models. The differences were admittedly small, but were consistently in favor of the judgmental approach.

Second, the main advantage of model-based methods seems to me not to be their accuracy but rather what Professor Klein refers to as the ability to "replicate" the model forecasts. A similar degree of accuracy has been achieved with econometric models over time, even though the economists operating them were changing. Therefore, unlike judgmental methods, the results reflect the model, and not the talents of an individual forecaster. Therefore, the reasons behind the track record of the model forecasts are clearly shown in the structure of the models and can be handed down to forecasters as a basis for developing the art. Testing models with different structures also provides a basis for evaluating alternative hypotheses on the economy's behavior. Such testing is of great value to judgmental forecasters. And, of course, models provide the advantage of ease of simulation. These attributes, not their relative accuracy, are the major advantages of the econometric method.

Third, the major advantage I see in the judgmental approach is a more flexible framework which is more conducive to predicting the unexpected or unusual development. Since econometric models have parameters reflecting average past behavior, they tend to lead to the consensus forecast. However, uncovering the unexpected or non-consensus development has the most value to business users of forecasts. Although models can be modified by judgmental inputs, the framework of the model user tends to focus his attention on past behavior, and the fitting of relationships to it. The judgmental forecaster is freer to weight more heavily the economy's behavior at present or in some selected earlier time, if he believes that is more appropriate. Also, judgmental forecasters are freer to ignore those official government data which they believe to contain unusually large errors.

Professor Klein's lecture concludes with several recommendations for improving econometric models. All of these tend to introduce into models some of the advantages of the judgmental approach. Professor Klein should be complimented as an econometrician who always recognized the important need to combine judgment with model results.

In conclusion, it seems to me that if the objective is forecasting alone, the judgmental approach, using models as one input, has the advantage. However, if the objectives are furthering our understanding of how the economy functions and contributing to the development of the forecasting art, econometric models have a decided edge.